A Sunday with My 2 Dads

Story of Lily Ma-Lewis
Written by Baba Ma-Lewis
Illustrated by Dada Ma-Lewis

CW01024936

For Lily, our sweet princess

Families come in many different varieties,
for us it's Lily and her two dads.

Most books we read to Lily show a traditional setup.
We wrote this book to introduce same sex parents in an
everyday setting, showing that the love of parents and the
daily lives of LGBTQ families are no different to others.

A SUNDAY WITH MY 2 DADS by BABA MA-LEWIS
Published by MA-LEWIS PRESS

Copyright © 2022 Baba Ma-Lewis
All rights reserved. No portion of this book may be
reproduced in any form without permission from the
publisher, except as permitted by U.S. copyright law.
For permissions contact: mail@neillewis.net
Cover by Dada Ma-Lewis.
ISBN: 978-988-75738-3-8
Printed in the U.S.
1st Edition

This is created by Lily Ma-Lewis, our two and a half-year old princess

This book belongs to:

....

Lily lives with her one dog, two Dads, three pigs, four sheep, five cows, six ducks and seven chickens on a farm.
Every weekday, Lily's two Dads work on the farm and Lily plays with her friends, but Lily is the one in charge of the family's "SUNDAY FUN".

Lily always has amazing ideas of how to have a wonderful Sunday.
One Sunday, she was Elsa, and she skated all day long.
Let it go, let it go......

Another Sunday, she became a cyclist,
and she rode her bike from home to the moon.
E.T. phone home......

On this Sunday morning, Lily planned another special day,
a 10 FUN THINGS TO DO day.
Lily and Go-go woke up early and wondered, "Are Dada
and Baba ready?"

They opened the door, Baba and Dada were still sleeping.
"We are running out of time," woofed Go-go.
Lily paused for a second and smiled, "I have an idea!"

She jumped on Baba and Dada's bed and started singing,
"Five little monkeys jumping on the bed......"
"One fell off and bumped his head......"

Soon after, Baba began cooking breakfast,
and Dada began dressing Lily......

......Baba brushed Lily's hair,
but Go-go still had nothing to wear......

......within no time, Lily put on her second shoe,
Dada was dressing like a KANGAROO.......

After a series of CHAOS......
"Fun Things to do number 1, a magical bus ride," said Lily.
The bus went round and round, up and down, and stopped
on a mountain top.

CLICK

Lily and her two Dads took a family photo,
where Lily was in the middle.
"Fun things to do number 2, Lily becomes a
butterfly," Lily spoke with a big smile.

Baba lifted Lily up high,
and she flew beautifully in the blue sky.
"Fun things to do number 3, we all get special treats."

Dada's favourite is fishing,
Baba's favourite is cooking,
Lily's favourite is drawing,
and Go-go's favourite is barking.

Fun things to do number 4,
Yummy, yummy, tasty food in my tummy.
"Who wants a lolly?"
"Lily, Lily, Lily."

Fun things to do number 5,
Lily's favourite time.
The biggest bubble time......

Floating...

and floating......

and floating......away..

POP! The bubble broke, Lily dropped into a lake,
......now it's swimming time......
Baby Shark doo, doo, doo, doo......

"Peekaboo, peekaboo!"
Dada ran to hide while Lily was counting down
from number five,
"5...4...3...2...1..."

"I won, I won."
"I caught you, Dada."
Lily opened the scarf,
It turned out to be Baba.

"Tweet...tweet...tweet..."
Lily sang along with the birds singing in the trees.

"Rainbow, rainbow, it's a rainy, sunny day......"
she continued singing whilst swinging.

Fun things to do number 6,
jumping and hopping until our shoes start
squeaking.

"Fun at the roof garden, that's the fun things to do number 7,"
Twinkle, twinkle little star...How I wonder what you are...
The family of three danced and sang
under the moon light and stars.

"Number 8, dinosaur." Lily roared.

"Number 9, Storytime."
Dada read, "There is a wocket in my..."
"pocket" Lily finished.
Dada continued, "and a findow behind the..."
"window" Lily followed.

"It's bedtime," Baba said.
"What's the 10th thing to do? Dada asked.
"Up and down, left and right, bubble bubble and
guggle guggle time," Lily announced.

"Now, it's bedtime." Lily kissed good night to Dada and Baba.
"Good night, my little princess." Baba kissed Lily's right cheek.
"Thank you for this wonderful Sunday." Dada kissed Lily's left cheek.

Avaiable on Amazon,
Barnes & Noble and other major online bookstores

THE PANDA FROM NANA

Written by Baba Ma-Lewis
Illustrated by Yang Liu

ISBN: 978-988-75738-1-4

A panda joined Lily's family,
a home of many colours, infinite love,
and plenty of fun.

But what does a panda eat?

Printed in Great Britain
by Amazon

84340440R00018

This is the story of a little girl called Lily and her two Dads, where Lily is in charge of Sunday Fun.

While Lily and her doggy Go-go were ready for their family adventure, her two Dads were still sleeping......

A sweet and funny picture
book from a rainbow family

MA-LEWIS

ISBN 9789887573838

90000

9 789887 573838